Y0-FZC-322

The AZTEC World

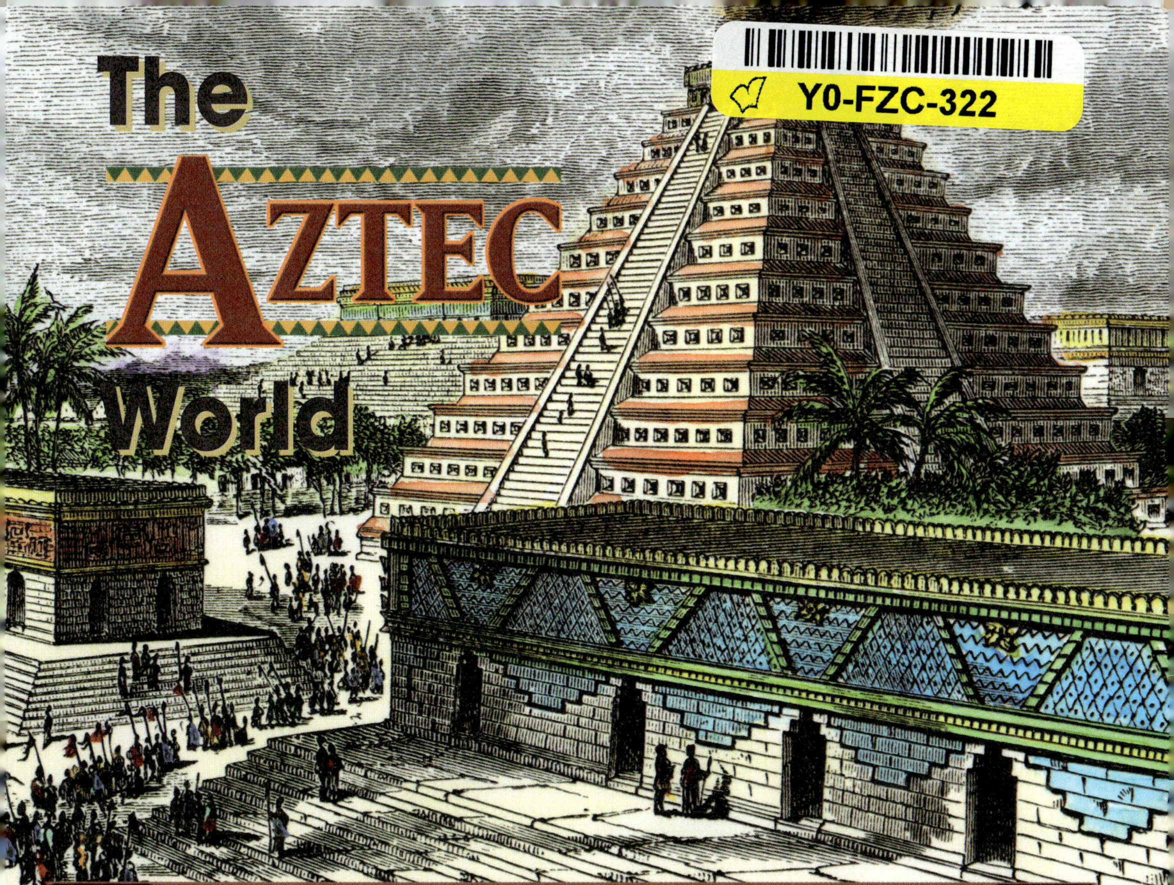

by Lisa Trumbauer

Table of Contents

Introduction

The **Aztec** lived long ago. The Aztec lived in North America. The Aztec lived in Mexico.

▲ This is the Aztec city of Tenochtitlán.

What was Aztec life like? What did the Aztec make? Read to learn about the Aztec.

Words to Know

Aztec

conquered

conquistadors

empire

explorer

island

valley

warriors

See the Glossary on page 22.

Chapter 1

How Did the Aztec Empire Begin?

The Aztec came to Mexico. The Aztec came to a **valley**.

▲ The Aztec came to this valley.

The Aztec built a city. The city was Tenochtitlán. The city was on an **island**.

Did You Know?

About 200,000 Aztec lived in Tenochtitlán.

▲ **The Aztec built Tenochtitlán.**

The Aztec **conquered** other people.

▲ **The Aztec had an empire in Mexico.**

The Aztec had more land. The Aztec had an **empire**.

People to Know

Montezuma I was an Aztec king. Montezuma I helped the empire grow.

Chapter 2

What Was Aztec Life Like?

Some Aztec people were rich. The rich people were nobles. The nobles had land.

▲ Aztec nobles were rich.

Most Aztec people were farmers. The farmers grew corn. The farmers grew other crops, too.

▲ Crops grew on floating land.

Did You Know?

Aztec farmers grew crops on floating land.

Some Aztec people were **warriors**. Aztec warriors used spears. Aztec warriors used bows and arrows.

▲ The Aztec used spears.

The Aztec believed in many gods. The Aztec prayed to the gods. The Aztec prayed for good crops.

▲ These are statues of Aztec gods.

Did You Know?

The Aztec had a sun god. The Aztec had a rain god.

Chapter 3

What Things Did the Aztec Make?

The Aztec made bridges.

▲ The Aztec made this bridge.

The Aztec made temples. The Aztec made pyramids.

▲ This is the Great Temple of Tenochtitlán.

The Aztec made statues. The Aztec made paintings.

▲ The Aztec made statues of their gods.

▲ The Aztec made paintings of their gods.

The Aztec made pictures. The pictures told stories.

▲ The Aztec used pictures for writing.

The Aztec made clay pots.

▲ The Aztec made this pottery.

The Aztec made jewelry.

▲ The Aztec made this jewelry.

Chapter 4

What Happened to the Aztec?

Spanish **conquistadors** came to Mexico. Hernando de Cortéz was a conquistador. Hernando de Cortéz was an **explorer**. Hernando de Cortéz looked for gold.

Spanish conquistadors killed the Aztec king. Spanish conquistadors killed many Aztec nobles.

▲ **Hernando de Cortéz and his men came to Mexico.**

Spanish conquistadors conquered the Aztec.

The Aztec Empire ended.

Summary

The Aztec lived in Mexico long ago. The Aztec built a city. The Aztec made pyramids and temples. Spanish conquistadors conquered the Aztec.

1200	1325	1438
The Aztec came to a valley in Mexico.	**The Aztec built Tenochtitlán.**	**The Aztec had an empire.**

1519
Hernando de Cortéz came to Mexico.

1521
Spanish conquistadors conquered the Aztec. The Aztec Empire ended.

Think About It

1. The Aztec came to a valley. What did they do in the valley?
2. What was Tenochtitlán?
3. Who was Hernando de Cortéz? What did Cortéz do?

Glossary

Aztec people who lived in Mexico

*The **Aztec** built a city.*

conquered fought and took over

*Spanish conquistadors **conquered** the Aztec.*

conquistadors Spanish explorers and warriors

***Conquistadors** fought with the Aztec.*

empire people and lands ruled by one ruler

*The Aztec had an **empire**.*

explorer a person who goes to new places

*Hernando de Cortéz was an **explorer**.*

island land with water all around it

*The city was on an **island**.*

valley low land between mountains

*The Aztec came to a **valley**.*

warriors people who fight for a group

*Some Aztec people were **warriors**.*

Index